THOMAS FITZSIMMONS is an American who is currently Poet and Professor of English at Oakland University, Rochester, Michigan. He has travelled widely, having taught at seminars in Pakistan and the University of Nice, and for a year at the University of Bucharest. His closest contacts, however, have been with Japan, where he was Fulbright Professor at two Tokyo universities from 1962–4, and worked in close co-operation with a number of well-known Japanese writers and critics in the compilation of this anthology.

JAPANESE POETRY NOW

JAPANESE POETRY NOW

Remade into English by

THOMAS FITZSIMMONS

First published in Great Britain 1972 by
Rapp and Whiting Limited
105 Great Russell Street London WC1

Printed in Great Britain at
The St Ann's Press Park Road Altrincham Cheshire WA14 5QQ

ISBN 0 85391 176 2

CONTENTS

PREFACE

TINNITUS BY AND BY
THEN CONSTIPATION

You who read prefaces know how it is 'impossible to translate poetry'. So let's talk about mysteries.

Given a certain sharing of assumptions, it does seem possible to translate statement with some kind of accuracy. Hence machines. Mysteries, though, seemingly at best can be invoked, imitated. Hence the maker. A distinction the remaker should observe.

Mystery is one of the words rejected in our time, itself a mystery, both the time and the rejection. Yet no other word more accurately focuses on points in time where/when persons and made things cross in such a way that the made thing happens, is lived, through and into.

Making possible such happenings is the business of Makers and their Powers. Human Powers. Most human. But most difficult for humans to deal with humanly—without reference to gods, goddesses, godishness, or to systems inhumanly abstract. Hence the jargon and posturing of the various Criticisms.

With a pantheon for reference, one that included at least some gods as playful and silly as men, mystery once was admitted to range high and low, contradict internally, present ridiculous enormities and sublime trivialities as well as the usual symmetries. Abandoned of gods and hooked on lesser systems, we tend to insist that mysteries to be mysteries must be profound, by which we mean worthy of jargon and gesture. But so much of what mystifies us is not profound that in the end we deny mystery just as we have denied Magik and Powers even while striving to become Adept.

I doubt very much that mysteries are carried intact across cultures by careful men whose profession it is systematically to describe, explain, analyse. Their commitment is to the reduction of mystery. And they have served us well. But ask them to preserve rather than reduce mystery, and the very dedication to precision that usually is their strength can betray them into such sublime absurdities as the couplet that serves as title for this note. [1]

[1] Rendering, by a Japanese scholar of impeccable training and intentions, of lines 25 and 26 of Hiroshi Iwata's 'Saturday Night Date,' on p. 67.

Science and scholarship seek first precision of item. Art tries for accuracy of pattern. To construct an effective pattern the artist will select and combine whatever items he needs and resort to any strategy or artifice that will serve to shape them. Call this activity invention or creation, it amounts to assertion that is empirically false: lies and the deceptions of artifice somehow woven into patterns that are valid—not mysterious? Magic, then. Magic more white than black, perhaps, but still magic.

There is magic in poetry. And mystery. And sometimes miracle. Who ever denies it should turn his attention to other things. There seems to be work for all hands. In turning mine to remaking of the poems in this book I've tried to make poems in English, never merely to describe a Japanese poem. I am less concerned with precision of transcription of detail than with fidelity to pattern and whole, the human vision vibrant there. Agreeing that no mystery should go unchallenged, I believe that no actual mystery should be violated, bent or reduced to fit some notion it has not helped form. In the dim regions roamed by poets the scalpel bites like an axe, and what elsewhere might be delicate dissection is here mere butchery. What of our living we do not understand, most of it, must be preserved as potential experience potentially understandable. That I think is why we make. And why we remake.

Many people have helped me remake the poems in this book. Rikutero Fukuda, poet and critic at Kyoiku University in Tokyo first suggested it in 1963, and together we worked over ten or a dozen poems before eye trouble forced him to abandon. Ichigoro Fujii, professor at the same university, has contributed encouragement throughout. Various Japanese writers, notably Kenzaburo Oe, Ryuichi Tamura and Shuntaro Tanikawa, helped me choose what should be included.

At noted in the text, Gary Snyder and Neal Hunter each entirely did one poem. Nanao Sakaki put one of his into English. (Both Sakaki poems included here are taken from a collection of his work first published by Bill Thomas at TOAD Press, Eugene, Oregon and are included with his permission.) Makoto Nakagawa helped with some, Takako Uchino worked on all of Jun Takami's, and Hidebumi Tanaka was consulted on at least two-thirds of the poems.

Teo Onuma, a young Japanese poet who writes in English

has been, however, by far my single most important collaborator. Without his work for me in Japan, this book might not exist.

I also thank Oakland University, Michigan, for a small grant of money, and a large gift of goodwill.

Thomas Fitzsimmons
Rochester, Michigan
1971

FAMILY PORTRAIT

Shuntaro Tanikawa (1931–   )

Water in a bowl
porridge someone ate and left
a wooden spoon
wildberry wine
underneath it all
a heavy wooden table

A man in rough cloth
sitting
strong arms
thick beard
eyes fixed
on the still dark fields

A woman
breasts heavy
hair rolled
work warm hand
on the man's shoulder

And a child
mud on his broad forehead
turns to us
as if surprised

The old ones
in a picture on the wall
are patient
beside the calendar
while a great dog yawns
at the door

Light glows on a simple altar
the night quietly turns to dawn

NO. 62

Shuntaro Tanikawa (1931–   )

Because the world itself loves me
(cruelly at times gently)
I can always be alone

Even when first I was given another
all I could hear was the world, its voices;
for me there are only the simple griefs and joys
I belong always and only to the world

Sky   trees   earth's flood of people
into these I leap
and that richness is me

But turn me to one person singly
. . . the whole world fades
there is no me

A CHILD AND A RAILROAD

Shuntaro Tanikawa (1931–   )

Another day and the child busy again
making a railroad   endless
railway drawn full down the road's
middle.

Busy every day child on
the endless way
white chalk rails reaching
but never reaching
terminal;
busy every day while people
in or out of love
clamber on/off real trains.

13

Child one chalking rails to no
where people peering over
hedges laughing or weeping
in/out of love.

One day a real train crushes the child
late sun hanging
red in white chalk like a terminal
where rails end.

LOVE

TO PAUL KLEE

Shuntaro Tanikawa (1931–   )

Forever
and all ways
just like this
together
for the weak
for those who love but cannot touch
for the lonely
we must make a song
one timecracking song
to reconcile earth and its heaven
rejoin the separate
merge the beat of one heart/all hearts
give back the trenches to the old towns
sky to the ignorant birds
fables to children
honey to the bees
the whole world to those who have no name

forever
all ways
like this
one song singing itself
in itself complete/completing
folding everything into one name
bringing peace between tree and woodcutter
girls and their blood
this chant and another
letting every thing be
and be yes
and be one
as the song is one
and for ever
and for all
for all ways one
that all the world should sing
and be sung

LITTLE BOY'S MARCH

Shuntaro Tanikawa (1931–   )

Tapered the penis
like a rocket for the moon.
Fly little penis fly
while It covers Its eyes.

Soft is the penis
like a tiny tiny pet.
Run little penis run
faster than *kiki* the snake.

Cold the penis
bud waiting for sun.
Bloom little penis bloom
let the honey run over the pot.

Hard is the penis
straight as a rifle. Shoot
little penis shoot
till all the lead soldiers fall down.

YELLOW POET

Shuntaro Tanikawa (1931–   )

Poet, yellow on a white toilet seat, forgotten,
sitting quite still yet anyone could see
he was dead: heart beat regular at 75 per minute:
breath stinking of gin and rice.
No mark on the body but his brain is jammed
with pingpong balls, source, one imagined,
of his inspiration. I slapped him on the back,
spoke a few friendly words, but he was too
absorbed reading the toilet paper to answer.
Just as I left a great gushing sound of water
made me look back: gone, the yellow poet.
Must have deliberately by mistake flushed
himself down (such an open, candid fellow).
Three o'clock soon. May blows gently against
the window. The world doesn't care.

STILL LIFE

Shuntaro Tanikawa (1931–   )

small table by the bed
                      a lamp
circle of its light
                      a clock
by the clock
              her glasses

clock ticks spectacles shine
looking I feel nothing

just wanted to mention the
few things   and myself
first mention and last

clock clocks on   I
am through another moment
and I
                              may
explode

THE SOUNDS

FOR JOHN CAGE

Shuntaro Tanikawa (1931–   )

Sound
                    flowpast
fast of noise not
trying to be a river
                    gone
just heard but gone
and there is a river.

In the beginning these noises trying
                              to be
absolutely new a river flowed too
fast too slow
couldn't   but caught
the clouds as a river would
                              and people
saw them and ran with them
                                      but
saw too as the riverbank trees burst

with blooms that the river of sounds
was a reasonless thing
                without spring
                without fall.
And the humble simple sounds weary
forgetting what to be
                flowed
naked as noise and made
                never knowing
a river   not caring
not trying   spreading   being
                simply
simply being.

Spring
        thenand
Fall and the sounds
        the sounds
were suddenly
        ignorantly trees.

Sounds that do not watch themselves
pulsing in what makes them live
                sounds
that do not make men dance
                no longer
make men weep   noise
disappearing into the world   into
people   singing
eternal as the cycle of the moon   un
noticed as the cycle of the moon.

Thus do the sounds go round.

MOON-CIRCLES/MENSTRUATION

Shuntaro Tanikawa (1931–   )

1.
In the body
somebody cooks   ritual dishes.
In the body   somebody sculptures
an unknown son.   In the body somebody
bleeds.

2.
God's palms
pierced while making
cannot forget.

3.
'So regularly in me are held festive funerals
for those of my children who are younger
than young, who cannot die or ever be hurt,
returning to nothing, mourned with gay colour.
The ripe moon falls. There is no one to catch
or accept it. I squat alone in a cold place
waiting for someone who will seed the moon,
someone to dare crest the cresting tide,
helpless myself to cure myself, to heal
a wound sacred to the memory of . . . I forget.'

4.
In the body
this body   the tide pulls
seaward whatever would live.
In the body   this body   lives
a sea. In the body   this body   forever
the moon calls to the moon.

GO

Shuntaro Tanikawa (1931–   )

Well
let's go   where
                        shall
                we go asks
my friend   the
poet Fujimari Yasukazu
                        go any
            where
just   go   here
it's damp it's
                hot   so
we'll go
                away we go
With Khrushchev   with
Kennedy with Nell Jackson
                                with
                                blues

away
we go   to
demonstrations
weddings   go
to vote   no
where   not   how
ever here so
go   all
friends   all traitors   all
bores   all
                go
let's all go
along the world's rim
                        round
we all go
            one
after another   round

let's
go through Africa through
New Orleans Frisco Tokyo
Heaven Hell let's
go
smoking
the best cigarette
is LM is
Salem is Real Molloka is
                 Hikariah
such freedom   Philip
Morris best
is Gauloise Marlboro Navy cut
Corona is
Hope
ah
hope
          rising
                      let's
                      go
with smoke rising
now   go
we can   walk
run   go by train
boat   car
Chrysler's best is
                 Pjo
        is
Simca
MG Crown   ah
such speed   is   Jeep
Ford Moskvich Rambler
Skoda ah
such freedom
freedom
          to ramble
to
go
          let's
go   where

WHAT WAS EATEN AT THE SOUTH POLE

Gyo Inuzuka (1924–   )

Gull big in the pot insisting he still has wings.
A seal, boiled and boiled, asking, demanding
'Water. One glass of water. Sea water.'
My guest sits quietly;
He might be dead.
And on the table (I can see icebergs
drifting by) my
whisky monotonously proclaims
'Born 1820, still going strong.'
It takes vigour to cut the soul
to just the right size, carefully, and fork it.
Wrapped in smoke, I eat
furiously, a demon.
And sometimes I almost shout
'Remember these, my canine teeth.'

FOR SPRING

Makoto Ooka (1931–   )

Dig up the sleepy sandheld spring
Put it in your hair and laugh
Foams of laughter rippling the air
Quietly sea warms the green sun

Your hand in mine
Your stone in my sky
Petal shadows deep in my sky

Buds shoot out from our arms
From the centre of our vision
Gold splashing circle

We are
Lake trees sun on grass
Or tangled in branches
Your terraced hair
Where the sun dances

A door opens in a fresh wind
Hands beckon green shadows and us
Roads fresh on the earth's soft skin
Your arms shine in a spring

Beneath our hair fruit
And the sea ripen slow-
Ly under sun

THE RETURN

Makoto Ooka (1931–   )

I have come back
In the end always the
Return in dead leaves

Tips of the sail of broken will
Flutter in her
'When I believe I am beautiful
I am more beautiful than beautiful'
My hard face cuts
Through wind like a knife
And I was always alone afraid
To be as gentle as I could be?

No
Always I was gentle
Not to only one person but
To Eskimos Berbers all
Whites all passing lovers

Always gentle
Light drifting on the surface of things
Was the pose I wore
I had no posture at all
Drifting like lips touching space
Drifting

Every single tree trunk gone
Only leaves to make a forest
I was the lightning rod in a stormy night
Nature's penis suddenly erect
Lanced me I let
It go all the way through me

Gentleness always
Badge of cowardice

I stopped seeing
When I stared at the thickness
Weight hardness of things
All sucked up to the surface
To become shapes

I stopped seeing
People
Seeing all
I lost sight of each
Desperate I jumped
Tried to fall into the sky
But always I drifted

Asleep
I rose drifting in the room
Oozed out of the wall
From the window I saw
The air my own shape asleep in my bed

All things reduced to shape
Their weight invading my sleep
Slowly I became purer
Became a thin pair of scales shining
Balancing in midair two hands
An excess of air on each

Back to the body on the scales back
Yellow leaves dip up the sun
Throw it back
Everything balances against its weight
Is double
Laughter I must have and swift feet
Gestures of a distant stranger
To make my own

Back to the naked wrinkleswarming hand
Wonderful
The return in dead leaves

ATTEMPT AT A POETIC SKETCH OF DEATH

Makoto Ooka (1931–)

Unstable wings
Soar up and down
In a brilliant sky
Down and up

Lovers move
Funereal procession
Death is never pretty
White clover must cover it
Memorial songs be sung
Hands raised to breasts
For all the lonely born of wombs
Disappear among gods

A finger very soft and friendly touches
    the transparent depth in a brain
An uncompromising blow

Fire rings
Lotus altars trembling to a breeze
Absurdity elegant
Unable to strike back
Ugly reconciliations

What gushes out when blood spurts
Runs with the blood through the body
Shapeless
Weightless
Scentless
Noiseless
Beyond touching
Everywhere
Half brother to words

Movement hides
That immortal enemy of time
Of words

Something in you reached beyond the furthest star
Long trail led and swiftly
I plunged into you
In a horizontal garden spinning violently
I caught a bird and
As it changed into dew-wet moss
I was impaled by an enormous past

reflected on the screen of a falling sailor's brain
Shirts soiled in dirty nightlong thoughts
Shammed death like a gull dying before the sun
And I fell deeper
Far above the farthest star
Your garden receded violently spinning
I grasped death in you
That's why you fled so quickly
To keep your death

In my hand is a hole
Seen through it the world is black
Violent volcanoes erupt incessantly

O gentleness
Intimate of violence

Death
Worse than any sin
A mistake

Mind's hammer no longer striking tongue hung low
This need sends sleepless
Wings over the receding walls
Searching for small words
Deep in the softest axis
Of this wobbly world

Only he who life-long walks on my droppings shall
Never see death

'MARYLIN'

Makoto Ooka (1931–   )

Death
Turns the film backward
A mirror

The sweep of her eye no
Longer reaches dream's crystal forest
Dim flames of death carry her bed
To a gentle white elephant or
A closed lead window
Hair quivering she lies now
On a dark mirror as on a breadboard
Above a quivering scalpel

No scalpel can reach
Soul's truth and image

Through history's tinted glass
Each August hill seems
A burning Calvary
Do not ask her where the thorns are
Translucent thorns and poisonous
Raised amid fatal praise
You doctors searching
In the body of America for capitalism's
Cancerous cells
Invading her sleep
You turning your faces away
Doctors do not write
In the stories of your lives
Marylin's name
Her death tells all there is to know
About you

Now
In this time
A tear tells all there is
To tell
All a naked corpse must tell
Honest as quivering hair while
Words can only skim death
For a pudding poem

Her eyes sink
Become lakes
Cheap films float there
Glimmering in the sun like
Flies on water
Broken light showing
Clear against black sky
Hollywood pale and bloodless

To die bleeding real blood
You have to lie naked

Marylin
Soul noisier than the world and more anxious
Timid as a shrimp's feelers
Mirror of womanhood
Your laugh
Sun and cactus
First announced a fairy tale
No Yankee had ever known
Then into the door revolving
Between sleep and waking
You went
And never came back
Starting on both sides of the door
A crazy game of tag
So popular soon it made of you
A gentle it
How then could you come back
Poems are pale now
Nations are villages
Windows secretly weeping

Marylin
Marine

Blue

THE COLONEL AND I

Makoto Ooka (1931–   )

Colonel my Colonel
It is I who loves you
Where are you going at 8 in the morning
School?
Colonel my Colonel
Love you because I love bombs
Big bombs and all
Possibilities rammed
Full and precise
Behind triggers
Love
All earthquakingly beautiful parts
Shattering together
And you like a bomb
Colonel my Colonel

How beautiful the cloud
Violent vertical leap to thinner air
Wonderful cloud
Blink
Seismometer
Break
Blink
Humanity
Break
Blink
O bird
Break
Colonel my Colonel
From dugout to schoolroom
Precise are your footsteps
And I love them
Your lectures put Descartes to shame
Should be transcribed into Latin leaflets
Engraved in Kunic and placed on altars

Sanskrit versions pressed to breasts
When death comes
Under the linden tree
Let him hear let him hear
He who before Columbus
Discovered America

Colonel my Colonel
Why make bombs
Why everybody knows bombs
Are made to be dropped
Disposed of
For peace
Always short of bombs
Because always short of peace
We must make bombs
Whistle whistle whistle whistle

Colonel my Colonel
When I held your daughter
Close in a rented room
Was it only to dispose of her
Only for that?
Colonel my Colonel
It is I who loves you
Love you because I love bombs
And you are a bomb
And must be disposed of
Dropped
Into Sanskrit poems
Into my own poems
It is an order

HOMECOMING

Tsunao Aida (1914–   )

Finally I returned.
To my desolate village.
Returned
Where my home had burned.
Wheat,
Wheat feeding on the ashes.
There I squatted
And emptied my bowels
For the last time
And fell along the earth
Like molten skin. . . .
Some wandering dog
Will take my shoes.
And I
Will rot into earth,
To feed the wheat.—
Grind the fat wheat
Into flour.

WORDS DEATH GONE

Yasukazu Fujimori (1940–   )

Suddenly   You'll Die
Die

Magnesium flash.

Before dark night wrapped in dark
A theologian lost his voice
A swollen penis lost its head

Purple-split lightning crackled above
Dark soil frozen cultivated
After rice harvest
Under fluorescence
A chimney pops out of the dark
Lights of towns and villages
Twinkle far
On a path among rice fields
One white coffin shines
Abandoned by the procession
A child weeps sperm and water
A hole in his heart
Its pleading voice muffled by tears
Falls among gravel
Ominous sound of wooden slippers
Wake sparrows asleep in the lightning
Flying higher yet higher they split
The bodies of mourners
With the edge of a razor frozen

The child smiles
Chewing on a tootsie roll given by his mother
The child smiles
Forgetting words   smiles

REVELATION

Koichi Kihara (1922–   )

Hiroshima: 1945: of the many women who died, the face of one, the skin only, remained intact on the ground

Mine is not a human face,
flesh pinned to piece of gauze
yet I can't stop crying
                    calling.

Uranium nestled in my teeth,
Plutonium squirming in my nose,
Helium sparkling in blind eyes;
the world now is nothing but a rock
             washed in a poisonous rain.

This is what's left of one human being,
this thing on a slip of gauze;
but the rest of me, scattered across
continents, calls
                 screams for its face.

Look! Listen! A uranium shroud
darkens the earth. A rain of helium
mocks silence of roof and window.
Son of man! Will you forever kill
your kind? Utterly and forever kill your
kind? Life now is the locust only
             crawling in the wilderness.

ME AND TRAINS

Hiroshi Sekine (1920–   )

I get on a train
and there he is
appears
from nowhere
ordering me around
newspaper
magazine
I buy them in bunches
he scans them
tosses them aside
is bored

doesn't like the scenery
hungry
thirsty
stop at a station
I've got to run for food
a drink
he considers the population
of my destination
ruminates on questions
normally ignored
how can people stand
such a drab town
back straight
like some pompous
minister of state
pest absolute
and inescapable
waiting on the train back too
more of the same but
as we pull into Tokyo station
he leaves
like a spook smelling dawn
pushes into the crowd
gone

CIVILIZATION AT NIGHT

Hiroshi Sekine (1920–)

We wanted above all
a pleasant plan
so we held the meeting
in a room that seemed
a replica of an old
old inn

When the committee broke up
I started down the stairs
but someone called my name
a housewife she said and
a critic how many of you
in all oh ten I see
I have just enough for third
class was she going to pay
our fare it seemed quite
strange she came on down
and handed me a magazine:
Civilization

Going home I had a
companion a woman of
forty-five or six but she
sat suddenly at the edge
of the road as if exhausted
so I stopped and asked
where do you live
just as a light hit her
full in the face who are
you to peek into our lives
like this so I ran
toward the light and found
some firemen who might
have been policemen disguised
but I had no evidence so
I came back.

A friend of mine a painter
dropped in I took his picture
fuzzing the focus checked the prints
told him I could make him
look even funnier but he un
rolled an abstract canvas from
under his arm I was ready
to laugh until I looked care

fully but this is *an outrage
on personal rights* it can't
be allowed and rushed out
to find a lawyer

Just like when Mother got sick.

PHALLIC ROOT

FOR SUMIKO, ON HER BIRTHDAY

Kazuko Shiraishi (1931–)

God if he isn't is
and laughs a lot
like people some
people.

Today a picnic
out where my **dream**
touches the sky
horizon I come to **carrying**
the phallus
the long white root.

Sumiko's birthday
and I gave her nothing
could have given her at least
the seeds of this God given root
seeded that faint small pretty
voice I can hear on the phone
would like to.

May I Sumiko
but forgive me
this phallus has grown with the days
and now is so solidly rooted
among flowers of sun and moon
that it will no more move
than a broken down bus
so if you should want to see
night sometimes seeded with stars
or some man roaring
down the road with a hot bellied woman
you would have to lean
far out of the bus and peer
very carefully.

When the root is rooted
phallic among stars among flowers
it is good to see
Sumiko
and the glow of the seeded sky
the strange chill of noon
pulls at our bowels and
what can be seen must be seen
quite clearly
and all must go mad
root without name or suchness
ageless root
known in itself only when carried
high on the shoulders
of men in procession sacred
and you can only tell where it is
by the noise
vague disturbance
commotion and curses and the beginnings
of riot signs of the primitive seed
still ungoverned by god
who often absent
leaves behind him void and the root.

Look
the root abandoned of God
walks this way
young gay and innocently
cocky yet smiling the smile
of experience.

Now it is many
a whole crowd of cocks
walking around
but really it is one
and comes alone
faceless wordless
from every horizon.

That
is the gift
I would give you Sumiko
to honour your birth
wrap you all up in it
that you might disappear
into the very will of the root
become yes itself
wandering endlessly
then I would vastly hold
and embrace you.

THE MAN WITH THE SKY ON

Kazuko Shiraishi (1931–   )

He wears the sky   heavy
.hat the sky
face hidden   and
from the neck down drips
on the ground   coming
this way along pavement.

Tomorrow is—
something like a dog?
No wagging tail   but
tomorrow is a today
that will not fail   a tail
that will be a yesterday.

He passes by.
Indecent tails curl
around today   its ribs.
He whispers something   what?
what is what?   what is
why?   Suddenly he falls
flat on his stomach   looks
up at the hat   but the hat
is the sky   and
looking up there is no
Crablike he tries to clutch
the earth   the sky slides
from his head, over his
face like a heavy hat, hiding
all but his teeth   clenched
hard teeth.

A little later he finds it again,
the sky, down around
his belly now, but heavy
a hat as ever. Face still
hidden, dripping still, he
comes this way along pavement.

No matter how long he walks,
this man with the sky on,
along the long way to today,
from the neck down he will always
seem just a man who cannot
sleep   walking   walking   walking.

THE PAST

Minoru Yoshioka (1919–)

He hangs an apron from his neck
                            thin neck
        man without will
                            without past
picks up the long sharp blade
                            moves
        from the corner of his eye
                            sees
        ants in column scurrying
the dust wriggling with fear
                            of the knife
        the bright flash of the knife
even if the thing to be cooked
                    were a pot
        a lousy chamber pot
                    it would scream
bleed through the window
                    into the sun
                but now something
                            quietly
        waits
offering the past: stingray
                    on the block
slippery wet spotted lump quiet
big   long tail hanging
    loose and long   reaching
                            seeming
down through the floor into
                    another place
beyond it only slick grey roofs
                in the winter rain
tucks up his sleeves
        stabs deep into its belly
nothing   not a quiver

                    nothing for his fingers
                                        to feel
            murder   butchery
                            without a response
                                without blood
            is too much   horrible   gives
                nothing
            braces himself   slices
                through muscle and gristle
            into darkness
                deep/empty
                spurting nothing oozing
                                        nothing
            occasional stars glimmer
                    die   in the gut
                    done
            he takes his hat from the wall
                            leaves
            and from the place hidden
                                by his hat
            from around the nail hidden
                                    driven
                            into that wall
            slowly steadily
                thick as time
                            heavy with time
            the red blood seeps and spreads

THE HOLY FAMILY

Minoru Yoshioka (1919–)

            A shimmering chunk of ice is shaven
                        one evening in August
                carefully
                                    chosen

                    by a mother & daughter
                        determined to sever
            the ancient lineage of
                        elm and snake.
    They smile and
                    an old man dies
                        strangled
    between the elegant motion
                of the mother's body
                    and the folds
                    of her gown.
    And the great horses   yellow teeth
    flashing   finish pissing
                    under lightening
        that splays the hearts of two
    women.   Out
        of a ditch full of worms
                        the old man
    returns
        glutton father   back turned.
    And the daughter   womb
        bleeding for the first time
                    shows the feet
                        of a wolf
    pours the pain of her virgin flesh
                    into the seeds of
    the black sunflowers
    of that garden.
        On a day when furniture
                        and the sun
    speak night
                    the mother fucks
                        a stranger
        on the bottom of the sea
    clutching his head
                    young octopus head
        into the sweat of her groin
    and father
        showing his golden teeth
                            nibbles
    a bit of ice.

BELLYFULLS IV

Nanao Sakaki (1922–   )

Stand up snakes! Bursting the basting threads
twined on betel-palms, you, leaf-veins of hungry panties
on the desperate banana tree, sliding down the papaya
trunk sliced-up sail you stake your life on, in loess
scorched by high interest keel of random rainfall stopping
your ears to the star-and-anchor menacing reef and roar
of breakers summer orange a burr in the throat

Caught on chest hairs of star coral bloodshot
from camellia, wolf-in-sheep's-clothing stones on roofs!
baring defiant bums the momentary crimson bank deposit
always glaring from the cliff of square of monkeys and the
pantomime, in a forest of pygmy ants turned rosaries on
the necks of dummy flowers that nod yes yes to neon

Waiting vine of false morality and watermelon
physiognomy, greasy with the mascara of cycads and yawns,
eruption should the bougainvillea culminate,

Take off bare feet of 'harmony'—noodles
whirling on the wave crests of a cherry blossom snowstorm
even pigs can't bear—camphorized bridal night swimming
through rice fields of inflammable heat,

After warm palm-vomiting current, northern
limit of pimp traitor to the world's time deviations.

Translation by Neale Hunter

BELLYFULLS No. 101

Nanao Sakaki (1922–   )

Emerald sky
Leprous sea
What wretched dreams I'm dreaming!
Always mooring a sampan—

I hope to get free of
Timidity just now breaking out,
Stripping myself soul's nappy,
It's a bargain.
At the end of a scene with your ghost
I went up the ravine
Came back thru New Year's spitz-smelling
Charred pile caressing evening calm.
Then spongy future peers
Into the morning mist of 'honeyed words'
But you can jump over it as crickets.

Eternity is supper for sows.
I myself Jack
Ate an overflowing silence in summer time
Pubic hairs of human history.
Devour a damp crater plus the placenta
Sink to the lake at mid winter
Sleep to satiety

There goes Xmas party of mice in the kitchen
There goes singing of ardent spirits on beach
There comes vomit to the eardrum
There comes a blizzard merrily

Happiness calls back
Bellyfulls of falling stone.
Let's have coffee, business and creed.
False red peppers come down silently
To the time table.

But you can smile if you could
Next is scabby calendar,
Tore off a sheet, it says 'I love you'
Take care of French pox in a crescent moon.
Naked teacher, misery carrier-pigeon,
A tower clock in a park
You and your stone image are going down to the sun.
Artificial flowers, or jets of waters, perfumes.
Hey skylark, higher and higher!
—you may fall down to heaven—

If you want to love something
It could be the wind of Greek letters
Or tomb of duty getting sober
Once more   ding-dong
A chimpanzee is the very image of grandfather,
Namby-pamby footprints,
Over there boiling hamburgers
Narrow lane of spherical clusters.

Translation by the Author

FROM 'AU I LU MAHARA'

Tetsuo Nagazawa (c.*1942*–)

Ne vu
Ka maa
yut
uru
so   gu
nhu

a ba mu   kamu
          umu   tumu
               himu   shishimu
                    kaimu   ramu tamu

```
        kru    ru ru
Sasan  ruined  wallways—
        varnished coffin lids.
uem nem
   nem sem rosethorn
tunnel. sandsick inner bark of stupor
rosethorn breath of lava,
        sea, earth,        slackened.


Chasing water ev. death by water ev
                    deep gorge ev
Ev of snow egg    making rounds collecting ev
Earth-axis ev
Stand up  tautly wrapping ev        nude ev
Scorched earth of reedfires,
                    sunflower slushy.


on the floor, on the snow,
fatty altar hands


ev nuuu
```

Translation by Gary Snyder

I WAS BORN

Hiroshi Yoshino (1926–   )

It was I remember a summer evening not long after I began to learn English. My father and I were walking in the grounds when I saw a woman walking white in the blue mist of evening sadly slowly.

She seemed pregnant and I stared at her belly imagining the soft movements of the embryo upside down soon to be born wonder of that.

As she disappeared I understood suddenly why to be born is a passive form and said to my father I was born. Puzzled look and I said again I was born passive form man is borne he does not do it. For me it was only a grammatical insight.

But he began to tell me a story. A common fly he said lives only a few days and once I couldn't imagine why it was ever born at all and told a friend who brought one for me to examine under a microscope. He said its mouth was utterly useless and its belly held nothing but air. I found everything just as he'd said except for the eggs. It's belly was full of eggs pushing up against its breast as if the unthinking repetition of life and death would choke that throat with sorrow. Lonesome glistening grains. I looked at my friend and said eggs. Yes he said enough to strangle her it would seem. Not long after your mother bore you and died.

I don't remember any more of that evening's walk. But an image swelled in my mind till it throbbed. My body small but filling my mother's pressing upwards against her breasts her throat my thin mother

---

NIGHT

Yasuo Irisawa (1931–   )

> address
> hers
> 40 and 1
> I
> went to
> 40 and 2
>
> home of a crippled baboon
>
> back
> along the 7 rivers
> black
> as fresh oils from a tube
>   the stars
>   fell
> stars fell and snapped at
>   my
>   shoes

                I
                carried
                        along the way
                        dried herring wrapped
                                    in paper

                        dried herring

                        herring

LOVE SONG

Ryumei Yoshimoto (1924–   )

> Even if an acrobat whose role it was
> to make men bite each other
> tried to put me onstage, I
> would never believe murders always
> occur backstage, corpses always are
> carried down through the pit to a cemetery
> near the mezzanine.
>   But the fellow
> who killed me is right there posturing
> on that stage, and the one I killed
> rollicks in the audience.
>
> From the wings I watch the pit
> closely. Onstage my torturer plays
> victim while my victim grows slowly
> old like any parent in the hall.
>
> Yesterday's love is today's
> sullen anger and hunger and the world,
> preferring murder and gunfire,
> ignores the tragedy in *my* mind.

They stare at me but do not see
my pain. I could scream, curse;
no one would hear. Talk as I
may alone and forever no one
will note what *I* say.

Should I forget to love, put me on stage;
if I am showered with praises and riches,
throw me away: if I should call, bring
wreaths and listen to my testament; when
I die, console the world . . . and if
I should mention revolution,
bring guns.

THE BREEDING OF POISONOUS WORMS

Kio Kuroda (1927–   )

on the four and a half mats of the room
our only room our home
my mother starts fussing around
now that you've been able to get
a job I can raise silk worms
again after thirty years
chops up something green
into a basket it's a shame
we haven't got mulberry leaves
but I've saved the eggs
late autumn eggs from
the year you were born takes
a bunch of sandy nits from the old
trunk carefully puts them in the basket
then squats there in front of it
now that you've finally found a job
silk worms again think of it

for the first time in thirty years
in the morning leaving I look at them
grubby in the basket no change nothing
don't worry they'll hatch soon
and as I come in that night from work
almost it won't be long now so
I try to be nice sure mom they'll
hatch tomorrow try to sleep
now but she just sits watching
like she's set for the night I
sleep dream of an ochre lane
under a brutal midsummer sun
and two long rows of mulberry trees
burning wild dead worms
falling soft plopping on the road
under the flaring trees millions
millions and millions of worms
in the morning leaving I look no
change but now they smell stink
like they're beginning to rot but
you'll see today they'll hatch we'll
be busy better buy some mulberry
leaves on your way back some
where my feet stop and I lean
against some sooty tree on a grimy
Industrial Avenue what the hell's
going on seventy years old and
still obsessed with a handful
of land lost so long ago mulberry
growing land hers ours nothing
but a fantasy in a grey head old but
my fantasy new of tractors on the land
is it her land they need does my
dream need hers begin there no
matter tonight I'll make her
sleep tell her a story of a fine new
collective far away in Russia
and while she sleeps her dreams
I'll dump those illusion breeding
worms into the nearest canal

on the way home I get some greens
and when I reach the door I freeze
sure now that the damn things
have hatched are in there right now
eating my mother a soft slithering
munching tide of worms nibbling
at her swallowing digesting I
rush in she smiles see see
they're alive and brings the basket
already some have crawled out to
wriggle around on the mats
brown an inch long   crawling
across the floor inchworms no
no same mud brown skin but
different antenna mutations maybe
of a thirty year obsession but they
look like those poisonous near-eastern
worms that feed on desert plants I
stiffen imagining the feel of them but
now I've got to tell her I choke
it out the revolution's dead here
mother revolutions are only for
far away places desert places and these
things aren't silkworms I've never seen
silkworms like these but as she
comes closer I can see worms in her
hair on her shoulders and she smiles
yes there's one on her face revolution
what revolution has your dream come
back don't worry chop some greens
you'll feel better I just stand there
no words already can feel them
crawling onto my bare toes but my legs
won't move and I take the green stuff
hands like claws and begin tearing it
                              tearing

IMAGINARY GUERRILLA

Kio Kuroda (1927–   )

Days and days of walking
a gun on my back
the road twisting
threading one strange village to another.
Beyond is a village I know well.
And to which I return.
Must return.
Eyes closed
it is there: shape of the forest
a path through fields
roofpeak
how to pickle vegetables
all the relatives
a scrap of farmland to haggle over
petty formalities and whitewashed walls
white always
a broken hoe and other people's soil
fathers and their fathers cringing into death
mothers driven off. . . .
I return.
On a secret path I remember well
I jump from ambush, rifle poised.
This is the season of revenge
keeping blood fresh in the old old wounds.
The village is beyond.
Here the road knits strangeness to strangeness
and I find nothing I know, as if in a dream,
alone on the road.
I ask the way to a house
and find silence:
walls with no windows
no doors.
Another house
no windows or doors.
No one.

No sound.
Now the road hides in a village the colour of . . . what?
Where am I?
Where does the road go?
Tell me, please.
Answer!
The gun in my hands again I face the silent houses.
But something is wrong . . .
the weight in my hands is wrong . . .
wood—a rod of wood three feet long.

HUNGARIAN LAUGHTER

Kio Kuroda (*1927–*)

Believe me
I was hanged
head over heels
killed
in Budapest where entirely a stranger
I was

Hang them
enemies of the people
someone shaking me
someone hitting breaking my head
saying
He's still breathing
cruel
not knowing that at nine this morning
I was eating salt salmon

How can they understand groans
in Hungarian
groans of hatred
Have they seen stomachs bigger than bodies

eyes blind legs
that run before
belly hands that leave
shoulders to strangle

I see the streets of Budapest headlong
I am hanging upside down
free streets are over my head
burning streetcars under my nose
the incredible burning of myself

Incredible
Yesterday I was trying to make
the wife of a friend
'No.' she said and
I hurried home raging
to throw myself on the bed
but
believe me
hungry Hungarians attacked me
eaters of wheat bread
I eat rice
and I know hunger
hunger of love and
the real hunger
more bitter than love

Vision of famine all over the earth
of the cities' deadly opened mouths
seeing for a moment
among chimneys and derricks
and dogtoothed trees
famine run wild
I too am forever hungry and blind
able to run only with legs
scratch with loose hands
I shake the corpse
looking for a hate object
drunk with my own execution

Then a shell knocks down the clock tower
the hands fall fluttering to the snow
time has vanished in Budapest
and so has mine
of whom should I ask the time
I must by tomorrow write
a poem about Hungary
Who is Lakoshi
that one hanging
Where is Nagy
gone lost
as I am lost

Walking in the deep belly
of a gigantic factory
on the breast of a wonderful kolkhoz
drinking a glass of socialist Tokay
where is her house really
is she living with someone
pretty house in the country
give me her body
body not spoiled by anyone
her body
her belly and breasts
No
give me
the gigantic factory
the kolkhoz belonging to no one
the sweet Tokay
pour the soup in a vacant belly
hot Hungarian soup

The winter of 1956
snow in Budapest
footprints on the snow
a stray child creeps up the hill
singing the song of the Partisans
Here is my home
When I enter a strange face stares back at me
thin dead face asking

Who is it
Rolling out I turn back turn back
a crowd of people like a walking snowball
march of the homeless crowds
march of blindness irregular steps

Streets deserted
what flat is that
you always keep
in the deserted streets
comrades
what flag is that
you carry
A snow flag
snow-white flag
Are you against the revolution
No look
flapping over my head
flapping over my head
awful miracle
Horthy's flag
whiter than snow!

Street corners blocked
tanks coming up
among them a trumpet sings
husky voice
cry on a white horse

Cry
bronze statues
Budapest city of bronze statues
standing so long
now they lay down on the ground
bronze lips mumbling
the old things were easier
to understand
who are the enemies of the people now
what should we do

I tell you what
just turn the turret
aim
fire at the counter revolution

I hate all counter revolutionaries
I hit them
again again again
What happened to them
I don't know I'm gone
in Budapest where
entirely a stranger
I was

Believe me
wise comrades
it is strange
very strange
I laugh
my corpse laughs
trembling corpse
that can't do anything but laugh
In Hungary
laughter of the pungent Chaldash

NIGHT

Toshio Nakae (1933–   )

Walking out of town a man
quietly strikes a match.
When the child finally sleeps
its mother takes it away.

Three times the night questions.
No one answers.
Seeing the silence off guard
a tree screams.

Somebody scurries by.

Everyone knows. Everyone
except the night.
Puzzled it persists: who?
Who? No answer. No . . .
And in that silence the questioner
too is lost.

MOON

Toshio Nakae (1933–   )

Face
Slipping down
Grey clay face
Modelled in a graveyard

Eye
Eunuch's eye watching
Ratmen caught tight
In the cage of time

Window
Of a factory in the sky
Full of machines
To shred neurons

Ledger
Balancing what is not
Known to a man of no merit
As he dies

Urinal
Finest porcelain
Sinking heavy as a boy
Pees and dreams

Womb
Old barren womb
Feeding no truth
Taking no mate

Betrayal
Of each subscriber
Life maker consumer
Ruined by made desire

Fish
Dead fish floundering
Like all the stars
In the music of silence

Cup
Big cup
From which man-made
Neighing men drink air

Ass
Pale ass of the Sun Goddess
Ass of rock
Of the gentle ancient nothing

Dream
Red dream of blood coughed
Up bubbling easily by a man
Already cold

Song
Song singing there are no
Songs—song of the dead
Gods

Hades
Our city
Where we live and die
Thin white city empty

SEASIDE EXPERIMENT

Hiroshi Iwata (1932–)

1.
With the girls   I
High on the cliff look   down
To the sea.   A man steps
Naked from the sea.   Spring
                    every spring
A blind man shudders
                    out of the sea
Testicles dropping
                    water drops.

We're at *Inamuragasaki*
                    Kamakura
But at every beach I've ever known
  Kamaishi Abashiri Kure Kuyakuri
                    one naked man
Arms spread   flung to the sun
                              comes
                              runs.
Look
How the wind ripples the hair on his legs
How his muscles flow
                    how dark are
Red his lips
The twisted fish hook tattooed
                    on his brow
On his shoulders a sea urchin.

2.
Hand in hand with these girls
                crueller than myth
On a cliff sown with cones   I
    Wait for him   the man naked

Understand.
            He is gentle.
                                    Feet
Hair   palms elegant though scarred
By the nets   the twisting of the nets
                                    back
Big enough to paint on.   Gentle.
From *Hokkaido* to *Kyushu* nowhere
Will you find a man more gentle
                            more free

Islands   you   these   all islands
                                    girls
Gathered in a net like islands
Once   for you   I tore off
My skin   to bind my poems.

But this man   this one running
Blind and elegant out of the sea
This one can sit in the yellow sand
Sit while we watch breathless
                        and count

Clockvoiced
Backward   from ten
To Zero.

TYRANNY

Hiroshi Iwata (1932–   )

1.
Under the cliff   air
Ran like water
Shadows were distinct in light
And fleece floated
The camera so perfectly focused
That the touch of fleece and the cool moss
Cool on the forehead
Crossed vision   spectrum in
Memory twisted like rainbow
Three men on three horses
Come softly this way
Soldiers
Franco's soldiers

A song   yes there was a song
Deep in the loudspeaker lustrous soprano
On off a song and
Suddenly birds leap high
Under the soaring cliff
Air smooth as unrolled film
Only hoofs
Come and go
Between our hearts and the screen
(entre la y calor)
Echoing
When the cold air enters our bodies
Spain at dawn
Disappears.

2.
Pure as a madman gone crazy
Obscene as a saint   thick
Beyond recall
Colder than crystal

Baffling as father to son
Son to father
More priceless often than eyes is
History

Bad conscience chooses a back road   always.
Is night's task
Ours
Merely to bet
Endlessly crouching
Shrinking
Flutter patter threading fears
Shadow light   shadow again?

Fumbling through a bushy hedge
Fingers and fingernails seek sounds
Jubilee Jubilay
Who was it?

A girl fallen innocently asleep
All over piano keys
Body ringing final consonance

Lines in my lower lip
Stains and freckles   holes
All over

3.
White paper. Paper white   bloodless. In a vast room of frosted
glass I stand naked. Naked lover and friends each sweats blue
juice bathed in dizzy artificial light dragging faint shadow

If at least our bodies were too transparent for them to see
the musicians behind the glass. Into the lightclapped roundroom
music from everywhere flows   in colourless scentless streams
condemning our girls

Seeming to fall they start to dance eyeless like jewels without
lips twinkle twinkling they dance Harlem Nocturne black voice
of no male no female black voice dull worn voice sings dizzy
darkness thickens but I am paper white no face burning red coals
no reconciliation with the dark torturers the grey glass that
stares shines in their busy sighs 'a blue tune'

4.
Dreams end in a rustle   audience
impatient for the curtain to rise
Rising with the tide small world   mine
Inflated to the limit

Fanfare

In clear consciousness
Trusting my sweat and blood to words
Against silence finally here
I say Tyranny
Tyranny comes

Silence
Orchestra long finished playing
Audience holds the breath
That one in the centre
Woman who reigns over all this
In whom the evanescent future waits
Singer   our singer
But she does not sing
Lo her dress is withered she
Opens her mouth   closes it and
With a scream no one hears
Falls

Please   Silence   Calm down   Listen
Tyranny is coming   there it is

In daylight gentler than night into
A present dimmer than dream that
Sings the woman comes
And your voice dies
Her throat is more fragile than a whisper
Delicate ears hair always protected now
Given to the wind but unchanged when she sings
And your voice dies
Never sing to the sea never
To the sky
Swifter than speed
Tyranny comes to soil tree and water
Tremble before it
Aim at its eyes
Tyranny comes sings the woman
And your voice dies

DAMN SONG

Hiroshi Iwata (1932–   )

        Morning eight o'clock
        Last night's dream
        Seeps under the train door
        Sings its song
        'Want to sleep?
        Hey. Want to sleep?
        Yes? Or No?'
        Damn song   Damn song
        I want to sleep   can't
        Can't sleep
              Difficult girl   wasted seed
              Sly mind and frozen love
              Square habits   sea urchin

        Lunch break   an old love

In a bill collector's suit
Sings its song
'Want to forget?
Hey.   Want to forget?
Yes? Or No?'
Damn song   Damn song
I want to forget   can't
Can't forget
        Difficult girl   wasted seed
        Sly mind and frozen love
        Square habits   sea urchin

Evening   six o'clock
Tomorrow's wind
Stretches dark gentle hands
Sings its song
'Want to dream?
Hey.   Want to dream?
Yes? Or No?'
Damn song   Damn song
I want to dream   don't
Don't dream
        Difficult girl   wasted seed
        Sly mind and frozen love
        Square habits   sea urchin
        A sea urchin

SATURDAY NIGHT DATE

Hiroshi Iwata (1932–)

1.
Phone call in late afternoon
sunny afternoon:
a girl   a date.

In the blue light of shop windows
seven o'clock   a scarlet coat
she sees me and smiles
                                          but
a wind   something like a wind
                          swells between us.

Water trembles in the glass as
she drinks   shop talk   friend
talk   health   the rain   we
babble like birds then   silence
                                          why?

2.

The thin tube of time is choked
with grime   you can puff
till your eyes pop   nothing
gets through.

Yet sometimes it's clear
then you blink surprise
back off   laugh   make
nervous parrot noises
cock an eyebrow to show
you can't be fooled   so
your ears ring
          as the tube closes.

3.

The wind again   head wind
If I face east, it's from the east,
west   it shifts to the west
What   whose   stubbornness is this?

We stare into the dark   strain
into the dark   there's no one there
no one to see   but if we both
close our eyes at once
                    the wind dies down.

It all started gaily enough
like a great electric sign
switching on   but what?
Streets at night   children
in the streets   soldiers in the
streets   Mobil Standard Oil.

What is it that darkens the stars?
Looms up between us and the sky?
What holds us both like whores
on the street? Shuffling whoreshapes?

MOBIL STANDARD OIL

SEVENTY NONSENSICAL LINES

Masao Nakagiri (1919–   )

My words are wrong
the monster's are strong
fear of torture (someone said)
all the women I have held
are like onions washed ashore
is there nowhere a woman real
sure as a Parker that never
needs shaking
my words sound wrong
the monster's are strong
wipe away thought and think
wipe away feelings and feel
listen all you like to the radio
weather reports international news
you can know nothing
cannot even be sure you are living
all seasons are the same

know the single unique thing (he said)
my words are wrong
the monster's are strong
where's the enemy where the traitor
nearest you you yourself
I know that
so is there anything you don't know
I know it all but not
how to say it
sinister laugh of a blackbird (hear?)
my words sound wrong
the monster's are strong
seek in a word no single meaning
in a rose no rosy colour
somebody grew a blue rose once
don't get mired in words
feed cats words fattened on mice
kiss dust that you may hope
but I doubt it (said someone)
things I say wrong
the monster speaks strong
Mohenjo daro Mohenjo daro
from the groin of a nude standing on her head
grows a tree
a man weighs dates on a scale
name of a city on the Indus
four thousand years ago
meaning Hill of the Dead
and kept on dying until just now
fitting name
my image for a civilization
tall tree falling toward dawn
what I say is wrong
the monster is strong
chasing time
's to be chased by time
never an excuse when late for work
prize the peaceful lonely heart
as if alone on a boat at sea
possible to be many and one at once

harvest and famine in the same moment
the things I say are wrong all wrong
the monster the monster is strong
water wanders among wines
light flows thinly on a frozen field stops
magnetic field enigmatic field
chunk of charcoal from which these my eyes
when will it burn all burn out
who yes who
will be responsible for 2 billion people
the monster comes quietly
Clyton why do you worry so
about what they'll all say

HEARSE

Hayahiko Tomi (1910–)

Hurrying into the hearse so I won't upset the mourners laughter
swells in my mouth like gas and my lips keep twitching. Have to
get in fast

Small streets sloping through a bright early autumn after
noon. People in black standing as I walked holding the memorial
tablets respectfully out from my chest. I could hear women
sobbing

Slow and careful onto the step then
I dive into the hearse hurrying
into the narrow dark   crouch
beside the pale oblong blur   one
coffin nailed shut   **holding in**
the laughter.

My old man's in that box.

I'm his footman and I'll foot it with him all the
way   right up to the iron door of the crematorium's
electric oven.

Dwarf gestures they want from me and grieve when
I provide them thinking I'm controlling tears not laughs.

They're all mixed up I'm enjoying everything looking
at the quiet streets through the rolling rosecoloured
glasses called Hearse happy as a kid in a subway
nose against glass discovering all the black tunnels

For the first time in my life.
And I still alive

Hey there   Make way   Make
way for the dead.

MOUNTAIN HUT

Hayahiko Tomi (1910–   )

One stone hangs straight down inside a door that creaks
    itself closed.
One dead twilight soaked leaf clings to the shoulder of
    the man who comes through the door.
One empty cabin.
One man.

Look
at his face   dark lips grey nose red green dappled
    forehead.
Heavily he sits eyes open violet eyes open.

Down from the roof beads of soot and grime hang
    into his face.
He bends to take off the heavy mountain shoes   lies
    down.

72

Tired.
Very tired.
Look
    at the eyebrows turning grey the melting face.

On the stretcher of sleep he is carried   where?
Back poor bastard into the pitiless alien light?
Up down up down some endless mountain trail?
Time worrying his heels like a dog?
Breaking him against petty cliffs until
    like a dog he drinks numb fingered
    the water drops under dead leaves?

One stretcher carrying his icy sleep returns
    to the cabin at dusk.
Is set down quietly on the bare wood floor.
No way to know if it has come
    out of a big toy box
    out of the edge of a loaf of dry bread
    from under the stopped clock
    from between the kisses smelling of milk

Yesterday weary he climbed on the last train.
Got out at dawn at a small station   eyes
    shut all the way.
Stabbed himself with the rusty needle of an early winter.
Yes.

But now surely he can relax ?
Door's shut tight.
The stone weight hangs straight.
Not even a finger could get in.
So light the lantern.
Burn a little wood in the fireplace.
Talk a little to check things out with the smoke and flame.

Really safe?
Surely no one
    could have followed him
    here ?

BIRD

Toshikazu Yasumizu (1931–   )

```
bird
          sleeping
deeply sleeping
               high
bird
          waking
soft awake
               high
in the sky
always
    and all ways
riding
               wind
high
     above earth
     above water
     always and all
               ways
flying
```


THE IDENTITY OF LOVE

Toshikazu Yasumizu (1931–   )

```
Kids
clamorous with chopsticks
demand the fish
turned over.
We never see
fish fleshless
upside down.
```

Bare facts
turned any way we
choose are bare
both sides.
This fish on the plate
bones
has nothing more
to give.
A thing waiting
for innocence to
pick it up and
turn it over again.

BIRD

Toshikazu Yasumizu (1931–   )

bird
you must be tired
                        bird
your blood has run
                        run
and soon will spurt
from the small flesh
                        bird
your freedom must
have crippled will
                    free will
that your songs
are sweet
                    I think
is but a lovers' dream
            that you are free
surely speaks our
                        hunger
only   bird

come to my hand
                    bird
I will comfort you
until and when with
    these same fingers I
        wring your neck

TREE BLOOMING

Tsuguo Ando (1919–)

between two pressing walls a woman
like a nasty coloured sausage appears bends suddenly
back through a flimsy broken window frame into
faint light black hair hanging straight down black like
a thick blooming tree needing no longer light nor wind
more like a spindle of black black thread and strange
to say to us the sky no longer is that presence
up there closing now weakly her eyes aimlessly plucking
one ornament from her hair trembling
ornament like a star in a tree and looking down
I see in the sky the tree like a spindle the star
in the tree a cloud like a leach swimming away
around the star in the faint light at the edge
of the city where broken day has surely two
slopes back bent body of the sausage woman
held up by a flimsy window back bent
body of the sausage woman holding up a flimsy
window fresh blooming of a tree in the broken
day of the broken world

NOTE FROM THE DEAD

Tsuguo Ando (1919–)

Hiroshima: 6 August 1945: 8:15 a.m.: mankind's
first atomic bomb printed on granite forever
the shadow of a man resting.

A rosy metallic sunglow creeps
over grey swamp now the earth
a million times faster than
we can work can make can clean
long it has been since first we
dreamed we'd wipe away that stain

long since the day we gave up walking
tall on two legs two feet arms shorter
now than legs we still refuse
to walk on four and putting both hands
flat to the earth as if bowing greatly
we crawl on our hands and knees
                        long
since the day when we first saw that
towering blackpurple mushroom cloud
in the rosy mineralled roiling sky
now our bellies are swollen our navels
drip oil
           and we argue that there is
too much oil or too little that one
has soiled where another has cleaned
laughing heavily painfully at our folly
till our ribs show clearly
                    no
longer do we hide our privates
no time for secrets what troubles us
now is what to do with these dark
red swollen dripping navels
                  will
they grow eyes noses hair

useless as upland riceweeds—
each morning gravest hour of the day
we check to see and only then crawl
happily on our hands and knees
in the rosy light of the sun

                              long
since we began to clean away that
stain ourselves that fouls the
earth

            long now since we lost
our home   the dark where it all
began

SLEEPLESS NIGHT

Toyoichiro Miyoshi (1920–   )

The midnight flame proves nothing
has nothing to say
groping in the crowding dark, is
merely part of the dark's vast hulk,
part of its claim, its right,
lighting only the edge of the antenna,
the everywhere reaching tendrils of night.
All we can know is the skin of the dark.

And our dreams are exposed like pebbles,
pebbles in a fast clear stream,
like the brains in a shattered head, spilled
guts, the sacrificial calf, burned leaves
and grass, the sick man chewing on
straw, the cottage of hate, the low flying

bird. Day after day we scurry along,
polishing pavement, to be summoned each
night to night's arena and run, run,
run from the voice that lashes our backs,
run to the cackle that tugs at our throats,
run from the shouts that mock us as our
questions are returned as answers.

And the darkness vast and swollen
swells till its claim, its right,
its bellow stifle the living heart
and we dash around our midnight
flames, pushing at darkness, pushed
by darkness, pushed, pushing, pushed
till we crumble. Then dead on the palm

of the dark we lie, like calves on
an altar, till it spits us into light.

PRISONER

Toyoichiro Miyoshi (1920–)

Midnight nothing no sound black
Cracked by the bark of a startled dog
Leaping at the cliff of sleep.
Ears cower deep into beds.
Beds floating in the clouds.

Lonely teeth scared jump around.
Hollowed voice warbles up
Down little by little I fall.

Two holes in the wall my eyes.
Glowing greenly on the desk
My dreams. A red star burns
High; a sad dog barks here
(from somewhere an echo barely).

The secret clears—my heart too
Holds captive a dog, pale
Sleepless dog called life.

SOFT DEATH BY WATER

Toyoichiro Miyoshi (1920–   )

Mackintosh on the wall.
Shell of a chained poet.
Link of gut full of images.
No sun touches my grin.

Sleep Miyoshi. In earth's
gangrenous crust, sleep.
Bald head propped up, drooping.
The road ahead stretches to the very
core of earth, narrowing, narrowing
like blue sky over a well digger
(he no longer sees).
Soft death by water soft
floating on timetides.

He leaves nothing but pen
scratches on a sheet of failure.
Seaweed cradled body empty
of sperm. On a deserted beach
one worn condom rolls.

One o'clock in the morning.

SMALL TUNE ON SNOW, IMPROMPTU

Choku Kanai (1926–   )

```
Who
        out of this world
                        tears
                        scatters
So many letters
            n
            d
            l
            e
            s
            as if a mind were spitting ashes
            l
            y
What
        compels you?
                        Like a child
shaking  his  head  obstinately.   S
                                    n
        quietly                     o
        quietly                     w heavy as muffled
                                            sobbing
From a deep hollow
```

LOOK/COME/CLOSER

Hiroshi Kawasaki (1930–   )

```
            Look this way please see
            the heavy golden hair
            a little twisted
            riffling in the wind
                    thick golden hair
```

just under the tiger's neck
about the paws
                come closer
come all the way
put your runny nose into
the damp slit of the tiger's
nose   deeply
                    come
those dry hips of yours
like crusted bread put
them here against the full
moon of the tiger's face
please   come   this way
closer   all the way

BARCELONA

Nobuo Ayukawa (1920–   )

Miro paints a sun:
        yellow candleflame.
I paint a Barcelona night:
        gin and sighs
        clouding lights of the Café age.

Greek you know and Roman
        politics; you with the wizard
        sandcoloured eyes. Europe
        is only the westward
        flow of this river Ebro.

You've just, think it now, come into
        a bar, an alley bar,
        in Barcelona, city of
        sun, city of night.
You're tired. Like me. A lonely trip.
        Let's stay the night.
        Here. This dream's end.

Miro's sun . . . I'd like to vomit.
     What colours . . . what are
     the simple colours
     that break us down?
Civilization is the colour of,
     oh, say, a 1930 sedan:
     colour of Arabian sand.

Look. Across the river:
     an Arabian fire.
In the heart of Spain of
     meditative darkness
     the desert lives.

ISHMAEL

Nobuo Ayukawa (1920–)

Why on earth was the law broken
blood's bond crystal shattered
the green pastures lost? Why?

How and from what place he came
he will not say
barefooted wanderer possessed
possessed of a certain charm.
Bearing the heritage of human
soul, faithful only to that:
Ishmael. Charmed.

But a soul needs tools as well:
mast   helm   charts   harpoons.
And this one, rapt in a vast dream
(not like some prodigal American
off to do Venice or Paris,
propelled by a farewell party; and
no cinemascopic adventuring
Ulysses solid in false armours
praising indecently flesh), this one
will never be weakened by climate or custom.

Ishmael on the Pequod
full of dreams
weighs in heavily against the ancient
law, old book, Old Testament.

And leaving land strikes for
not Europe's darkening clouds
not Asia's final angles
but the very core of the sea itself
pounded core where myth is
made of fate and wave   wind
and faith. Place of visions place
of terror   deep   leviathan.

Ishmael
whirled and beckoning
dancing the human breaking dream
the deeps that sucked at you
suck me.

AT THE BARBER

Ryusei Hasegawa (1928–   )

Going down slowly
very slowly
I came to the hulk of the *Chokai*
covered with seaweed swirling
blue, green;
the battle cruiser *Chokai*; I
had seen her last in '37
being finished up in Nagasaki,
tall in the Mitsubishi shipyards;
here she lay on her side
in the silt, stripped of her guns;
I figured her for 20 million *yen*
and started slowly slowly up.

This in a barbershop in
Shinjuku, where Tokyo
drinks gambles and whores,
from a dark wild face
against which the razor,
smooth western razor,
glistened as it moved.
Then the barber's bony
fingers slid down down
slowly and out of sight.

BIRDS

Taro Kitamura (1922–   )

I love birds. Water life is foolish.
And the things that creep on the ground,
Wriggling through dust, are base. Butterflies,
Flickering against grass, bees, winged ants
Live but a portion of an hour, a day. . . .

Held, a bird is warm—
Silken feathers, knowing eyes—virile,
Lonely and virtuous.
Yet their legs are the limbs of a man
In agony.

The piled clouds rub darkly together
And the rain floods down. Heavily. Slowly.
Suddenly, there: blue for a moment,
And into it swings a bird. . . . I

Am human, a creature proudly erect
With ideas and images;
A meat grinder spewing hate and desire.
And so I like the limbs of birds—
Rigid even in life.

ONE IN A GRAVEYARD

Taro Kitamura (*1922–*)

Why knock on the iron fence?
A magic wand
Wouldn't bring him back.
He died in the summer
1947
Vomiting parasites like sausages.
(wet gravestones recline;
this fog is the coldest)
Pain
Humiliation
Hopes torn up—of these he died
And his eyes turned up
So.
No gentle lust
No lazy coffee
Nothing
Allowed to defile his crest.
Corpse of a dog.
(boring day with a dead architect)
Ah, who says his mask forever
Stares at us with bronze eyes?
Nothing but pale bones is heaped
Under the heavy stone
In the dark soil
Only white teeth rotting
(once they bit pomegranates)
Who, then, turns the stone over
Nails all bloody
Searching for the shadow with a rusted spade?
(that summer morning the coffin wheels
creaked and stopped on the wet soil)
He is dead now.
The grave digger has given him a number.
All over.
He sinks in the evening fog
A dog beside him.
Good-bye.

HALF AN HOUR IN THE EVENING

Saburo Kuroda (1919–)

Take the rice off the stove, break
some eggs, beat them, pause
for one shot of whisky, fold one
red paper crane, chop onions—
stuck in a kitchen smaller than a
towel half an hour every night.

Seasoned housekeeper,
drunkard,
father,
playmate for little Yuri too;
half a day at the neighbour's and
she's ready for company, has lots
to say, lots to ask.

'Read to me, daddy—'
'Untie this string—'
'Can you cut this, daddy?'
While I'm trying to get the eggs
just right. 'Hurry, daddy;
potty, daddy.'

Fed up I toss some seasoning
in the pan, knock back
another shot, little Yuri's
getting fed up: 'Can't
you cut this for me now,
daddy? Daddy, hurry up.'

So I blow: 'Leave me alone!
Do it yourself, dammit.' But
this little girl's got a temper
of her own: 'You cranky, drunken,
nasty old daddy.' And I let
go one big hand solid across
her bottom.—Tears. Howls.
Lots and loud. Very very loud.

Then
quiet,
the beautiful time:
the father gentle, kind:
the daughter soft, sweet:
the two of us at the table:
eating together
face to face.

NOTHING BUT A POET

Saburo Kuroda (1919–   )

That fine longhaired richrobed doll
in its glass case its world
or even that bright red sweater
of yours you can't just give
them away of course I understand
in this world there are simply too
many obligations complications
and you yourself you can't just
give yourself away I know
complications obligations are
in this world harder even than
in that of the doll or sweater. Much
like a kid who wanted just
what he shouldn't I go alone
walk the dark streets home
windblown bunched.

Before putting out to sea before
each long voyage a ship I'm
told is scraped clean of old
barnacles the last trip's leavings.
Once I thought to be a shipwright.

But I found out. I'm no
maker of swift clean ships
honed for each voyage. I'm
nothing but a poet.

NOTHING MORE TO BE LOST

Saburo Kuroda (1919–   )

Even if more had been asked
I had nothing more to lose.
Leaves blown into the water
Flow down with the current.

Once, in a boat on the sea of death,
I could do nothing but stare at the sky, seeing nothing.
And once I sat still by a friend on a tropical island
As he raved through madness to death.
Now looking at this swollen city,
Safe in the window of a white building,
I doubt that my way has changed—or its end.

Fate crashed upon my head
Like a girl hurling herself from a roof,
And I turned over to meet . . .
But it was not death.
Who lifted me, drew me?
You. A young girl.
Whispering,
Offering
All I had lost.

AUTUMN IN CLAREMONT, CALIFORNIA

Shozo Kajima (1923–   )

Fog rolling in from the valley,
San Joaquin fog wetting the evening
of a small town, and a twig
from an old grey Eucalyptus ghost
falling soundless on dark concrete.

Movie: a great cliff, beautiful; a hero,
heroic; and each time he teetered
on the edge of the cliff a lady beside me
clutching up, muttering, 'Oh my! Oh no!'

More fog, streetlights hanging heavy,
a little bent; moist leaves fallen
under my feet; a library, a book, voice
of a poet, lonely, weary, whispering:
'Just as I have been forgotten, those
who forget me will be forgotten; you,
haven't you forgotten that bright moment
at dinner once with those who now
no longer remember you?'

Going home, no, going back to my
room above the garage, suddenly
I hear myself saying to the fog:
'Enough, damn it; go away; clear up;
You smell like a Japanese bath.'

RED FRUIT/PATIENT

Jun Takami (1907–1965)

        sleepless
        congestion of trees
                at dawn
        when the pain starts
                again
        a red pomegranate shatters

BLACKBOARD

Jun Takami (1907–1965)

        Afternoon sun shines
        on white curtains
        of my hospital room.
        Like a classroom.

        When I was in Junior High
        my favourite English teacher
        erased the chalk on the board and
        books under his arm
        left the classroom with afternoon
        sun on his shoulders.

        I'd leave life like that
        wiping out everything with one swing
        saying 'So.'

TRAIN THAT WILL NEVER COME AGAIN

Jun Takami (1907–1965)

The dark train has left
taking as if erasing all
the few silent travellers.

The newsstand is closed.
Vacant platform at night.
Even the swallow's nest is empty.
The lights extinguished
the railway men gone.
For some reason I am still here alone.
A dry wind blows;
dust billows on the dark platform.
That train will never come again.
No point in waiting.
It will never come
I know it.
Knowing it I cannot leave.
I need to know death.
I stand in a nothingness worse than death.

Rails glisten like sharp knives
but since the train will never come
I can't die on the rails.

PEBBLE

Jun Takami (1907–1965)

please don't kick me
let me sleep
            in this place
I only want
to sleep

WHEEL

Jun Takami (1907–1965)

in a sunny happy place
a wheel   rusts
            small green fruit
is about to fall never
                    to ripen
a bulb buries itself
            deeper down

SOMETHING TERRIFYING

Jun Takami (1907–1965)

Something terrifying approached.
I ran. It chased me.
As I was running
it passed right through me
and left me behind.
What was it?
It ran as if I were chasing it.
Ran as if afraid of me.
What
I asked a man passing by,
can you tell me?
Death, he said gravely
through false teeth.
I thought him affected.
Only those who don't know death
talk of it.
But I don't know death.
I went into my inn.
The grey-haired clerk greeted me surprised.

I felt he hadn't expected me back.
The maid asked nervously where I had been.
I walked the corridor, slippers slapping,
reminded of the footsteps of whatever
had chased me, passed me, left me.
My room seemed far away.
So far I would never reach it.
In the stinking corridor I wondered
Wasn't it life?

LOST BADGER

Jun Takami (*1907–1965*)

When I was a boy
a naked badger with a *sake* bottle
used to come to the town liquor store.
Meeting often
we became friends
but when I had grown up
the badger had disappeared somewhere.

When he was drunk the badger
would dance or disguise himself
as a pretty young girl.
I'd clap enraptured.
That's how to trick grown-ups.
What fun it must be to trick them.

Abruptly sober the badger told me
No. You've got it wrong.
I don't disguise myself to trick anyone.
I'd never deceive them for any reason
but my own pleasure my own amusement.

Look at cherry trees.
They don't bloom for anyone's sake.
Isn't that great?
Their blossoms never show the hardships
they know.
Wonderful flowers on dirty branches.
A beautiful disguise isn't it?

I child did not get what he said
I see it now.
He must have been lonesome too.
Now I understand but the badger is gone.
He will never come back.

DANCING DEMONS

Jun Takami (1907–1965)

Don't tap your chopsticks against the bowl.
You'll summon the hungry demons
and they'll eat up all your rice. Long
ago my grandmother told me so.

Old now I rest quietly after dinner
making no noise at all. No matter.
Suddenly demons strange demons appear.

Snow outside but they leave no
footprints and their feet as they move from
the garden to my room are dry.

Plump healthy little demons clearly not
hungry living a better life than I
sick old man gaunt as a hungry demon.

Why have they come? To soothe me? These
merry devils are even more hideous
than their famished pale thin kin.

Frugging around my bed playing xylophone
with chopsticks on my ribs. Strange
sound they say and lean down
to listen pressing ears into my chest.

Then screaming fear they rush from the room.
What could have scared them. Fierce fearsome
demons. What could have scared them? Me.

POPPIES

Jun Takami (1907–1965)

Already under the ground.
A dog pees up there over my head.
It's all right.
A bird picking around with his little
beak tickles me way down here.
Soon roots of trees will creep
into my chest. But I like
to know how pretty it must be
around my grave.
Plant flowers
like the ones around Van Gogh's.
When I made my pilgrimmage
to Auvers there were flowers everywhere.
And in the wheat field by the tomb
wheat field he himself had painted
red poppies danced with young wheat.
Plant me red poppies too not
white. White poppy seeds give
opium heroin
deaden memory.

GARDEN

Jun Takami (1907–1965)

1: grass berry
a small prayer sleeps
behind leaves

2: prayer
can be sealed in small boxes
like jewels; can be hidden
in a little heart

3: red maple-shoot
small red hands held out
to the sky
praying shapes unaware
praying
beautiful

COFFEE/NO SUGAR

Hisahi Ito (1923–   )

Shop door opens:
two men in,
a little smoke out.
'Lay him out
by the fourth round. . . .
I'll have beer.
Coffee for you—right?'

Getting dark; bar
signs begin to flicker
in the evening,
in the gentle hearts
of men, my kind.
Am I looking
at the new champ?
Above him and his coffee
a poster pronounces
time and place.

'Remember your right, boy.
Your right': the fat one,
gulping beer.
The young one is
silent, taking his coffee
black/no sugar.
His 'right' barely moves,
quick/sure, when he drinks.

I pay: go out: leave
the fighter's world.
A fine May evening,
floating, refreshing.
Crossing the tracks
I pace slowly
towards the arena.

VERONICA

Hisahi Ito (1923–   )

Under Spain's hard midsummer sun
blood-rite and bitten breath freeze
a mob to watchfulness—death's
simplicity, living's blur caught
held here by a master's brush.

Out of the painting out
of dust gold rolled one
great black brute bull

Charges: Veronica:

Sweep of scarlet   dance
of a man slim spinning
deadly now   steel-poised
gone as two curved horn-
knives stab   shadow

From one painting to another
each stroke is sufficient
necessary. Skill saves
the matador. His skill and
Goya's.

Distantly the voices swell.

LOOKING AT A CHILD'S FACE

Akira Shimaoka (1932–   )

must be alike
father's face child's face
smell of a sleeptime crime
pulling out the child's hand
clutching the line of destiny
mine the father's hand holding
a song of death
sad contract of the jailbreakers
giving mouth for mouth
nose for nose eyes for eyes
so this head may become that

on a small plot in another's
garden suddenly a sun flower
starts to laugh and in the dim
evening sky a sea snake swims
while everywhere blood suckers
twisted lips pouting wander
look my daughter each small
hope pulls the trigger in its breast

PALMWAYS

Akira Shimaoka (1932–   )

I Look:
>On my palm ways wander.
>Are their lengths fixed? curves plotted?
>Must I go that way only
>that way see only that way
>you, the sea, the setting sun?

You Look:
>From your palm
>me.
>Hands fold and the ways tremble.
>Who set them there?
>We clasp hands and the ways
>mingle   darkly   darkly
>but can never merge.
>Who shaped the way?
>Our fathers? Who
>shaped theirs?

>Sometimes a blade sliced
>across a wrist
>will hide the paths in a flood
>of blood trickling into a new
>red selfmade way.

But soon a dog like god
will lick off every trace of blood
and the dead way is shamed
by the light.

We Look:
all of us
from different places
with different eyes:
look at one scene, touch
one man, but tell it
differently: '*I* saw. . . .'
At night our ways seem to
melt together; lies
are more beautiful than light.
But even when a boy holds a girl
in his arms
they go their different ways.

TRAVELLER'S SONG

Shiro Hasegawa (1909–   )

What was it
half sunk half seen
bobbing in the sea
ahead of Columbus?
A leaf.
And what
did Noah's dove
sent a second time
bring back?
One soft olive leaf.
Before me on this sea:
a window

ink bottle old desk
newspapers.
Dove. Dove.
How many flights you've
flown for me. Again
now. Up. But
you'll come back
as usual
bringing nothing.

WATCHMAN'S SONG

Shiro Hasegawa (1909–   )

High pressure low pressure
                                I
always wear
a raincoat   and wander
with a lantern   I
                    am a watchman
      Faint trace of young animals
on the pavement   look
out virgins   I
know where these animals go
                                I
              am the watchman
Lighting a lamp in the basement
of an empty building   every
one's gone home   I'm proud of
my lineage, watchmen all as
                                I
              am a watchman
Negro soldier darker than night
walking by   I
can see   as you walk by
the white

```
bones inside you              I
                 am the watchman
Sleeping              master
sleeping         everyone is
sleeping       and all is well
all's well for now       signed
                              I
                 the watchman
```

BED THAT SMELLS OF SUNSHINE

Hitoshi Anzai (1919–   )

I don't get much loving from this man,
but plenty of kids girl/boy/boy/girl,
at least one too many by any count. No
yoghurt at all for whoever sleeps late.
And at TV time, one's got to sit on wood.

Oh, he likes my sheets: lies on his belly
and sniffs: 'Hey, even in the dark
they smell of sunshine.' Bites my
finger, wedding ring and all. Doesn't
hurt (you'd think *that* finger would
react); I even like it. Naked bodies
have strings in them. We tangle ours
up, jingle them loose. Afterwards
I like to watch him smoke in the dark.
He looks wicked in the little light.

I know all about him and his secrets:
the sexy magazines (he must keep them
at the office now), the carefully wrapped
dirty pictures. You have to watch this kind
of husband. He intends to keep me
just a little hungry. Damn him.

MORNING: PHONE RINGS

Hitoshi Anzai (1919–   )

I flick on the washer: the phone rings:
buzz of his razor like a far off saw:
eyes closed I see his head, shoulders,
chest, hands, fingers.
                              Always the same
words: 'Lonely; but I slept well. Wish
I could eat breakfast with you.'

And the girl, back turned, hooking her bra?
If he didn't call, he wouldn't have to lie.
But mornings he doesn't call I'm
nothing but a busted clothes washer.

I work, hard, to bring yesterday
fresh, clean into each day, spread
the sun over my garden. Proud:
                              my children
off to school hours ago, small tight
boats in the wind; and by now my
husband has caught his bus, stiff/frowning
in a stiff/clean collar.

Every few weeks he takes me out to town,
my lover, sticks his fingers into my ears,
my mouth, and anywhere else he likes,
flips me over, turns me inside out.

DRUM FOR A LULLABY

Takuyuki Kiyooka (*1922–*)

A Sunday morning
about the middle of the 20th century
                              to be loved
              the damnedest surprise of all.
He runs
runs
and over the surface of the sea
like a song rubbing
inside his skin
hears a music that will flow
long after he's dead.
What we call history
isn't big enough.
That shadow there . . . born of
what mammal?
And that fear
last thing to leave any room
leaving earth in flames
casually biting off the nipples
of the sky . . . that mummylike fear
beginning to move, what?

He jumps
jumps
into a cloud
like a secret shelter,
gropes, finds the fingers
of a sleeping child.
Such peace . . .
what is its source?
What the source of serenity.
Eyes closed he yells
'How am I loved? Who loves me?'

DON'T GO TO TOKYO

Gan Tanigawa (1923–   )

Right in the teeth of the evil
of my native place I found
a town   capital   all muddy
colour of narcissus and strange
sound strange talk gentled
and undulant   no
not the rack of revolution
but sell the wagons gather cedar

and the woodcutter's daughter
all in tears will
play on a keyboard of stones
songs of a newborn land

out past the jumble and vomit of railroads
on meadows quieter than stars
beaten clear of the crows of despair

But morning is a fragile   fragile
glass   so   don't go to Tokyo
build here   build homes

And onto the mosscool mats
bring sailors farmers and miners
all the disgraces infinite disgraces
In our eyes our look is the capital
of a world green under ferns

the inside of the hurrying hoofs.

VOICE

Masami Horikawa (1931–   )

The edge of the sky
swings up, springs up,
for the sky often must
pull up its hem to be sure
it is still the sky. And
sometimes it tumbles down
only to climb still higher.

Something hotter than heat
but born of heat
stands up and walks
always just at the edge
of the sky, where earth
and heaven push apart,
and birds that will not
die in the hottest heat
flutter and endlessly fly
that circle.

Whoever licked and tanned
the beasts with his tongue
is not of necessity our
father or mother. When
the walls of the town pulse
out and fall the Voice
comes from you to me
swelling quietly.

TOUCHING A BOX OF DREAMS

Masami Horikawa (1931–)

In the diamond valley where an old sailor nods,
in black burner pipes mixing gas with air,
was despair distinguished from experience?
Is it only a big fist that bulges the pocket?

Each morning's paper is crammed with letters.
Readers write. But hope now is an empty well.
If we could be just, only, what we wished,
my thanks alone would shrink the earth.

Clutching the red claws of the birds, one by
one we rose from the pit. But rid
of handcuffs we put on watches. The husband
sleeps by his wife, his children.

Stuffed with drugs, blood, flowers, and sap,
there is no difference under the skin. Stars
overhead, the sea in our shoes, carbon
everywhere singing the iron mirror of the past.

Where pink clouds tangle with a new river
I'll come visit you. And I will
hang on your neck all the rubies I've
scraped together—on that morning when your past
any past, everyone's past becomes one past.

NIGHT

Minoru Nakamura (1927–)

night night why do you tremble your lips
fragrant as fruit too mellow supple
your body why do you sigh why hide
your face in the damp of your hair

rotten and falling something is rotting
everywhere falling and night will not
wait for dawn turns itself pale rises
becomes tree with boughs and leaves

but the sands of the dunes whip in the wind
scattering leaves shattering bark till all
things fall and night is a pulsebeat drawn

from death and burial and too must fall as
the twig hanging against January's sky
so we try for sleep in one another's arms

CASTLE

Minoru Nakamura (1927–   )

From the pit of a dry canal
street climbs steeply to
sky, rushes past warehouses,
racetrack, stretches straight for
the sea.

Out of the swelling city white
lava rolls down to the sea
and next to that flow of garbage
looms the Modern Castle.

The City has many faces but
around each high neck, each
low ankle, crawl in a black
endless chain deep deep
driven pilings, bridgesticks.

What do we look for?
What does this Castle
keep for us now?

TOP

Kikuo Takano (1927–　)

never still
love
solitude
nothing works
you can only be still
spinning vainly
around yourself

but
spinning
what dizziness
as if losing some
fine spun essence
of self

and still
spinning
out what load
on to what already
bending
barely enduring
watching
self

RIVER

Kikuo Takano (1927–　)

Up. It would—wouldn't it—be good to rise?
But for you it is always down. Today
(yesterday, yesterday, yesterday . . .)
you claw and tear at the channel that holds you,
wanting . . . yes, not to be a river.
And the drive and swirl of that madness is fine.

But finer still is the suffering you hide.
What is this you would claw away?
What are these limits you cannot tear away?
Earth?—Not even that.
Something . . . something I think about
think about always whenever I cross you,
knowing you suffer as I suffer.
And I look at the sky, the sky
you, falling, would seize. I look at clouds.
Birds. Fishes. The whirlpools of your despair.
And I know, whatever the sky is, whatever
a fish is, I
am as you, river:
channelled by failure,
caught on the rocks in my depths.

A BOY AND HIS MOTHER

Kikuo Takano (1927–   )

    'Is it the sea roaring?'
        The sea has long been dry.
    'My ears ringing?'
        Only you would hear.
    'The train?'
        Gone long ago.
    'Someone's snoring.'
        Everyone is listening.
    'Fire. Fire roaring.'
        There's nothing left to burn.
    'The sound of the sky?'
        The sky was first to die.
    'What is it, then?'
        I don't know.
    'It's the end!'
        No. It must be endured.

'The sound?'
 No.
'Time.'
 No.
'Oneself?'
 No.
'What endures what, then?'
 I don't know. No one does.
'What do we do?'
 I don't know. Endure, maybe,
 that you don't know.
'That I don't know!'
 Yes. It must be that. Endure
 just that. Until you die.

'FOR YOU'

Kikuo Takano (*1927–*   )

Like two mirrors
facing
we gave each
the other
identically.

            Do you
remember when we first
met horizontal on dry
grass
            we saw the same
sky same clouds one
hand gently touched the
other
we didn't even cry.

Away from
everything towards
nothing
you said
I believed.

        Silent we
knew everything
quietly
but didn't know at all.
You mocked your love. I
mocked mine.

REMEMBERING A POET NAMED BLAKE

Koichi Iijima (1930–   )

1.
Once
there was a poet named William Blake
who sang Peggy and Susan and Kate,
the tyger, and the cloudy sky. Once
there was a poet named William Blake. . . .

Did he burn inside? Had
time a shape
for his hands? Could he,
during the days
bent over etchings bent
over by Catherine, could he
feel it?

Announced
The Marriage of Heaven and Hell
What is now proved
Was once only imagin'd. . . .
So said Blake
eyes wide in the dark.

Do you remember?

2.

I stretch and grind my brain for
words. To find in words . . . mere
twinkle of a season warped for
memory? No
               I, weighing this
glass in my hand as I would weigh
an ovary, and receiving signs
colder than iron from other
poets not content, not quiet, I
have remembered the name of Blake.

That name remembered can
save these hearts more easily
moved than sands, ease our
hunger for power, soothe our
sufferings with the suffering tree.

3.

I had planned a poem of fire
denouncing the U.S. Government.
All I have now is a simple
cry: Stop killing in Vietnam!

A few shaky words.
No poem.
Realizing even if I
could pump blood into a poem,
could ram all of myself into
words, I could never get through,
could never reach them,
—Pharisees.

4.

Alone, I pour whisky into
myself instead, pour it on
the fire, powder, deep
in me; trying, failing
really to know, to hear,

the guns at dawn in Saigon,
to realize the G P U.
                    Tonight
again I will fall on my knees
head loose like the men shot
at dawn in Saigon, fall
rocking into the river
of sleep. And I will not
dream!
                    Serene I will
sleep on the rotting straw
of the hacking board.

Daylight catches me flat
in a schoolyard, scrambling
under machine gun bursts.
I see myself. And far away an
icon, glowing; then, suddenly
it flows, all wispy and
white, right at me, right
through me, arms and legs.
Bullets chase me everywhere,
but can't hit me: like
an old faded movie, exhumed
for TV: tense but ending
happily.

5.
On the street today I met
an American painter, maker
of blue geometry, yellow
mirages, misty whites;
takes for his bible, *Moby Dick*.
Had been in the U.S. Air Force
but crashed in training.
So many things he wants
to talk about: politics,
'the floating world' of sex
for sale, acres of blue
balls, the bombing of

oriental villages.
He'd
had a buddy who touched
a kind of ecstasy while
looking down on a burning
village. But the painter
of blue balls preferred
to lay on his back reading
Blake.

6.
How do we do it? How do
persons manage to float
in this too bright space
between steel and neurosis?
Me, I've tried to catch and hold
the sky of my childhood.
Blue sky. But I can't make
the words come right,
can't make the ink flow
steady on the page. And I'm
left with a sky cold and
thin as a negative.

On that film I can see
a football field in Butte,
Montana, but no miners,
no Montana miners deep
in their holes. A bulldog
wearing a big '63' looks
back at me.
Naked arms,
shoulders: lots of those:
movie queens, sirens.
I drink my whisky.
Somewhere in the Congo
soldiers of a new Foreign
Legion swig some beer
while tripping the triggers
of machine guns.

Nothing new in all this,
except me, my anger and
pain. A private affair
between me and the U.S.
Government. So I send
this out in the dead of night.

A certified letter, routed
through Vietnam to pick up
a little blood in route.
Otherwise pale. A most pale
letter, as befits us, a most
modern people. Proof
that in civilization as in
poetry, there is no progress.

Pale letter for paled critics.

7.
Blake would grieve
as we grieve.

'Rintrah roars and shakes his fires in the burden'd air;
Hungry clouds swag on the deep.'

So he warned. And would
lament. Keats too.

I will listen to the bee's song
on the sterile hills.
The fields shine with
dead dry grass.
Treading the soft soil there
I will grieve for tomorrow
as well.
                And I will remember
now and then that Blake
has been. I will love
red and yellow roses.

117

And go in sorrow.
                    The last
cold winds of winter will
have me, have us. Blown,
floating, we will land
somewhere.

SEEING THE INVISIBLE

Koichi Iijima (1930–   )

Poor fellows:
stuck with mud when ever
they would think snow.
The first image swelling
under the lids
is the soul's colour.
Fire & Snow.
Frosted glass
walls the dark rooms
under eyelids: cold
water washes there
bloody knives red
gauze, a pageant of
bird feathers, crowded
petals tremble in night air:
ordinary women in common
skirts and jackets, one
at each window, become
green streaks, thick foliage
melting on the dawn's tongue.

Poor fellows
feeding nothing but sick
dreams, they will die too,
and having befriended the grave
will not rise with the wind.

Clever guys are clever
even in their graves. As if
they had never loved women
they will hate to be grass
trampled. We will die too,
but with our sensual dreams
unspoiled.

Clever guys know everything.
We are new born. Will—
will we?—learn to sort
things useful from useless?
Will the tip of my tongue
see more clearly than eyes
into snow, trees, grass, buds?
Eyes closed: way back
in the orchestra that young one
I love poises a twinkling
triangle, waiting the moment.
She too sees the invisible;
keeps the fire.

STRANGERS' SKY

Koichi Iijima (1930–)

The birds are back
Pecking the black void of the earth.
Circling up, down
Round the now alien roof-top.
Lost . . .?

The sky buries its head in its hands
As if it had eaten stones.
Broods.
Blood it cannot bleed veins the air
Like a stranger, circling.

119

SEER

Ryuichi Tamura (1923–   )

Voice
Sound in a birdcage
at dawn
Silent
Before I could hear
what was wanted

Image
Shadow in a lifeboat
at sunset
Gone
before I could find
its source

Dawn voice flying
to shape our sky
boat-shattering image
weaving horizons

My thirst pulses
in the nooning sun

THE THREE VOICES

Ryuichi Tamura (1923–   )

From far away, very far, a voice
softer than any whisper
louder than all shouting
deeper than time's waters
deeper than oceans
than the sea in words

breaking through lost seas only a poet knows
slicing earth's coldest air
sinking the most delicately poised armadas
ruler of our kings and the city of our feelings
remaker of dead seaman and of our boredom
Voice from far off, very far

> Because we cannot sin
> we are mere numbers
> a sum of fear
> declaring lust   declaring lust
> and cannot sin
> Because
> we are not single
> not individual
> we are the crowd   the mass
> we are mass itself

Through tears it comes, through a single tear
poorer than all the poor
dearer than all things dear
fiercer than heart heat
fiercer than the loss to us of the man crucified
than the love in words
slicing lost loves only a poet knows
sparkling in steaming cataracts
flowering in the driest throat
invader of our energies and our flesh
destroyer of our faith, our kisses
It reaches through tears, one tear

> Because we cannot end in love
> we are an invention of passion
> things of passion
> symptoms of crisis   symptoms only
> and cannot end in love
> Because
> we are not alone
> we are the crowd   the mass
> we are mass itself

Voice from beyond time, this 'only time'
time with a future darker than all pasts
a past brighter than all futures
sharper than God's grace
sharper than the light of a crack Express
than the time in words
slicing lost times only a poet knows
kissing the palest cheeks
lighting emptiest horizons
usurper of our corpses and our empty stations
perjurer of our science, our blood
Voice from beyond time, this time

Because we cannot die
we are an ad for immortality
a no-death advertisement
a means of consumption   of exploitation
and cannot die
Because
we are not single
not individual
we are the crowd   the mass
we are mass itself

When finally that voice is heard
My mother will be born of me
When it is heard
These our dead will feast on vultures
When at last it is heard
My mother's loins will give us death

INVISIBLE TREE

Ryuichi Tamura (1923–   )

On the snow I found prints
and for the first time knew
the world of small life,
birds, beasts in the forest:
squirrel, footprints down an old elm.
across the path . . . gone among firs—
no anxiety, hesitation, nowhere
a question;
a fox, coursing straight down the road
through the valley north of my village—
my hunger never drew so straight a line,
never in my mind so smooth, blind, sure
a rhythm;
a bird now, prints clearer than her voice,
claw-marks sharper than her life,
feather-flicks frozen in the sloping snow—
my terror could never tremble to such pattern,
in my mind never such a pagan, sensual,
affirmative beat.

Suddenly—sunset
big on the summit of Asama.
Something not known has built a forest,
pushed open the mouth of the valley,
split the cold air.
Back in my hut
I light the stove
thinking an invisible tree
invisible bird
invisible small things living
rhythm invisible.

FOUR THOUSAND DAYS AND NIGHTS

Ryuichi Tamura (1923–   )

To make a poem
even to begin
is to kill
tear into and out of
much that was whole.

To hold the trill of a single bird
tongue trill trembling on a page held
we cut from the pulsing sky
silence of four thousand nights
radiance of four thousand days.

Needing the tears of one hungry boy
we murder the love of four thousand days
grief of four thousand nights
in the wet cities   midsummer harbours
coal pits and smelters.

To catch the terror of one stray dog
staring at something we cannot see
driven by sounds we cannot hear
we poison the fancies of four thousand nights
cold memories of four thousand days.

To make even a piece of a poem
is to kill much
that was whole and loved.
For us, no other way to quicken
the dead. No other way to go.

MEET AGAIN

Ryuichi Tamura (1923–   )

Where shall we meet again?
Where?
Old friend of death. **Old**
friend of mine?
                    Noon high
in the city, shadows slipping
behind pale doors, gone.
All twisted memory gone, lost
in a city's colossal lie.
You don't remember how I
smiled, whispering 'desolation
smiles.'

Looking, I see a dead volcano,
sexual windows, order of a kind
but without a sun. After noon
in the park, afternoon dying dry
in my hands, summer ever
cracked between my teeth, earth's
dark darkness against my chest.
                    Where did we meet?
I, a boy, seventeen, given to
prowling alleys. Sudden rain. A
hand on my shoulder. A voice:
'Earth's crust is rough, friend.'

HYMN NO. 1

Taro Yamamoto (1925–   )

God
put me on Jesus
was his shoehorn
dazed
I ran a thorny path
like an ostrich worn
torn

Ah God
my rebel tongue
damned me
used me
kept me on
Walk I shall
walk for how long

Dusk on the highway
gateway to sorrow beyond
Clouds burn in the sky
float like intestines
A *tofu*-vender's horn
turns the dusk
into a place of terror
In such a place
where soul is wasted
streets people trees
All seem the writing
of a coarse mind on a crude wall

God
frenzy in His hands
dances high above
finally to descend
And I on earth
become a hole
not yet a snare

not so audacious yet
But I am a deep deep hole
waiting to capture my
God alive

Legs stretched toward sun
head deep
in the centre of the earth
upside down I
am the shadow of a *noir devoir*
too small to be a pylon
twentieth century design
but if one day
a God should trip
over my foul shadow
and fall
I will laugh in its hole
deep in the earth
Then I will
join the disciples

That is to say, **God**
this time I
will put You on
Eyes closed blessed
hear Buddha's laughter
deep in the hole
beautiful
appropriate to a snare
Around this life
a gentle light lingers
Christ and His God
are captured in Judah's mouth
but like a dry well
It still digests a small small anger
and O
I am
a hairy worm
five feet six in the earth
trembling

I put on
light is my shoehorn
God
and He
shocked
wove of Himself a mushroom cloud
to tear up sky
like a bandage worn
torn
Now at the end I
shall be with You
naked drunken

God
I am
small
so small
a worm
Let me confront Thee
smash into Thee
and become at last
a miserable accidental
smudge

HYMN NO. 2

Taro Yamamoto (1925–)

I'm critical
magician awake

another margaret withering
a goldfish dies; beautiful

answer waited
tell your love

I'm young & idiotic
drunk fond of bad things

help
generous reward

resurrect O Lord
on a wooden horse in the park

redhaired woman caught shoplifting
go and tell people

comfortable in cages
Alulu Khan flies with a dog

quick!
quick everyone everyone suffering

in a ribbon ends this path
ah those of girls dancing like butterflies

quick! sea run dry
sardine children why not wail

among the trees on the highway
daughter of Pegasus

in love don't come
send money

start disciplines
beg relief

song of a running rickshaw
memories of a perishing father

dying at last
ancient gods goddesses

under the plantain the old decay
the young in a racket meet

go all dreams
mere genital we already

sobering up in a cell
sad the moon cracked behind bars

O le printemps

I'm critical
magician awake

no die now all you
le printemps shoot again down infinity

so be it but weep now for now
for reasons beautiful this prayer song

BIOGRAPHICAL NOTES

Tsunao Aida (1914–). Visited Nanking in 1940, then worked for a publishing house in Shanghai. Returned home in 1945. His collection of poems, *A Lagoon,* received the first Kotaro Takamura Poetry Prize. Works for a publishing house in Tokyo.

Tsuguo Ando (1919–). A winner of the Yomiuri Literature Prize for his essays on poetry. His publications include *Literature of the Visionary.*

Hitoshi Anzai (1919–). His publications include *The Florist's* and *Handsome Man.*

Nobuo Ayukawa (1920–). Returned from fighting in Sumatra in 1944 and joined the Waste Land, once one of the most influential groups of poets. His publications include *Poems* and *The Making of Modern Poetry.*

Yasukazu Fujimori (1940–). His publications include *An Abnormal Fifteen-year Old.*

Ryusei Hasegawa (1928–). Runs an ad business. His publications include *Tiger.*

Shiro Hasegawa (1909–). He is now more of a novelist than a poet. His publications include *Siberia Story* (novel).

Masami Horikawa (1931–). Present editor of *Modern Poetry Notebook.* His publications include *The Pacific Ocean.*

Koichi Iijima (1930–). His books of poems are *Strangers' Sky, My Vowel* and *Microcosm.* Well known as a poetry critic he wrote *Introduction to Surrealism* and *Essays on Art for Exorcism.*

Gyo Inuzuka (1924–). Works for the Asahi Press; accompanied the Japanese expedition to the South Pole as a reporter.

Yasuo Irisawa (1931–). His publications include *Happiness and Unhappiness.*

Hisahi Ito (1923–). Runs a publishing company in Tokyo. Member of the Waste Land.

Hiroshi Iwata (*1932–*). A well-known translator of French, English and Russian. His publications include *Warfare of the Brains.*

Shozo Kajima (*1923–*). Teaches at the National University at Yokohama.

Choku Kanai (*1926–*). His publications include *Hunger, An Inordinate Ambition* for which he received the H Poetry Prize (the best known prize for poetry in Japan) *Suspicion, Small Tunes on Love and Death,* and *Songs of Innocence.*

Hiroshi Kawasaki (*1930–*). A poetic-drama writer. His publications include *Swan.*

Koichi Kihara (*1922–*). Staff member of *Shigaku.* He won a Ministry of Education Prize for a radio drama (1957). His publications include *Portrait of the Stars, Poems,* and *Some Place Some Time.*

Taro Kitamura (*1922–*). One of the most promising post-war poets in Japan. Works for the Asahi Press.

Takuyuki Kiyooka (*1922–*). Works for the Japan Central Baseball League and is also a film critic. His publications include *Frozen Flame* and *Days.*

Kio Kuroda (*1927–*). Engaged in the agrarian movement after the War, ruined his health and came to Tokyo. His collection of poems, *Anxiety and Guerrilla,* was awarded the H Poetry Prize.

Saburo Kuroda (*1919–*). His first collection of poems *A Une Femme* was awarded the H Poetry Prize. His publications include *Thirsty Heart* and *With Little Yuri.* Works for the N.H.K. (Japan's broadcasting station) and is also known as a poetry critic.

Toyoichiro Miyoshi (*1920–*). He is a member of the Waste Land whose publications include *The Prisoner.*

Tetsuo Nagazawa (*1942–*). Sometime editor of *Rega* and now editing *Psyche,* he is a Harijan. (A Sanskrit word meaning 'Children of Hari.' A Harijan as a rule belongs to a loosely-organized communal tribe which works at various jobs and shares its wealth.) His publications include *Death Script* and *Sand Sleep.*

Toshio Nakae (1933–   ). His publications include *Time in Fishes, Songs of Darkness,* and *Refusal.*

Masao Nakagiri (1919–   ). Works for the Yomiuri Press. A member of the Wasteland, his publications include *The Poet of Crisis.*

Minoru Nakamura (1927–   ). A lawyer whose publications include *Tree* and *Silent Song.*

Makoto Ooka (1931–   ). He teaches at Chuo and Hosei Universities. His publications include *Art minus 1* and *Poems.* He is also a noted art critic.

Nanao Sakaki (1922–   ). Also a Harijan, his books include *Four Poems* and *Bellyfulls.*

Hiroshi Sekine (1920–   ). His publications include *Introduction to Modern Poetry.*

Akira Shimaoka (1932–   ). One of the few poets in this collection who does not live in and around Tokyo. His publications include *The Giant's Dream* and *Idol.*

Kazuko Shiraishi (1931–   ). Born in Vancouver. Her latest volume of poems is called *Tonight is Nasty.*

Jun Takami (1907–1965). Died of cancer in 1965. He was both a novelist and poet. His publications include *My Burial, Poems, From the Depth of Death* and *Tree Group.*

Kikuo Takano (1927–   ). A teacher of mathematics. His publications include *A Top* and *Existence.*

Ryuichi Tamura (1923–   ). Formerly an editor of a publishing house in Tokyo. His publications include *Four Thousand Days and Nights* and *The World Without Words,* which was awarded the Kotaro Takamura Poetry Prize in 1963.

Gan Tanigawa (1923–   ). He no longer writes, but edits a magazine called *The Universe of Words.* His publications include *Poems* and *Merchant of the Earth.*

Shuntaro Tanikawa (1931–   ). Was given a Japan Society Fellowship to the USA, 1966–67. His publications include *62 Sonnets* and *Loneliness of Two Billion Light Years.*

Hayahiko Tomi (1910–   ). Won the H Poetry Prize in 1956. His publications include *The Beat's Way.*

Taro Yamamoto (1925–   ). Teaches at Hosei University. His *Gorilla* won the Kotaro Takamura Poetry Prize. Other publications include *Walker's Prayer Song.*

Toshikazu Yasumizu (1931–   ). A radio-drama playwright. His publications include *Songs for Existence* and *Bird.*

Ryumei Yoshimoto (1924–   ). Joined the Waste Land in 1954. He is now an influential social critic. His publications include *Poems.*

Hiroshi Yoshino (1926–   ). His publications include *Vision and Method.*

Minoru Yoshioka (1919–   ). Works for a publishing company in Tokyo. He won the H Poetry Prize in 1958. His publications include *Still Life* and *Monk.*

DATE DUE

MAR 2 1977			
FEB 1 0 1979			
FEB 2 3 1979			
DEC 2 1 1979			
FEB 8 1983			
APR 1 3 1986	WITHDRAWN		
MAR 1 1 1995			

GAYLORD — PRINTED IN U.S.A.